Dynamic Programming

An Elegant Problem Solver

D1210893

Dynamic Programming

An Elegant Problem Solver

William Sacco
Wayne Copes
Clifford Sloyer
Robert Stark

JANSON PUBLICATIONS, INC. Providence, Rhode Island

Material based on work supported by the National Science Foundation and produced by the Committee on Enrichment Modules, Department of Mathematical Sciences, University of Delaware, and Tri-Analytics, Bel Air, Maryland.

Copyright © 1987, Janson Publications, Inc. All Rights Reserved.
No part of this publication may be reproduced in any form without written permission of the publisher.
Printed in the United States of America.

94 93 92 91   8 7 6 5 4 3

Contents

The authors wish to thank Jane Melville and June Sacco, who helped to produce this monograph.

Preface

During the past several decades many new mathematical methods have been developed for finding optimal (best) solutions to problems. These methods are used by investors to enhance profits; by physicians to treat patients; by governments in hopes of reducing energy consumption or avoiding wars; by athletic coaches for better training programs. The methods have colorful and curious names, such as exhaustive search, greedy algorithm, branch and bound, divide and conquer, linear programming, dynamic programming, etc.

As yet, no one method is best for all optimization problems, and thus today's problem solver should be familiar with many of these methods. In this module, we introduce dynamic programming. Invented by Richard Bellman, a famous mathematician, it is a simple, yet extremely powerful method for solving many optimization problems. For example, in the early 1970s, dynamic programming was used to optimize the California Aqueduct System, purportedly saving California taxpayers millions of dollars. We hope that the reader will gain some skill at applying dynamic programming and some knowledge about its foundations. The reader should also develop an appreciation for the power and limitations of modern computers.

Part I
SHORTEST PATH PROBLEM

A. Brute Force Style (Direct Enumeration)

To put certain facts into perspective and to limber up your mind, try your hand at answering these first two questions.

1. How many seconds are in a year? (Write your answer in scientific notation.)

_____

2. If a computer can do 10,000 additions in a second, how many can it do in a year? _____ In a century? _____

In a thousand years? _____ In a million years? _____

Figure 1 shows a map of several city blocks and the minutes required to travel each block. One path from A to B is highlighted with slashes. We call this path NENE, using E for an EAST step and N for a NORTH step.

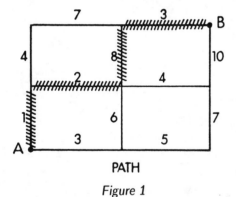

PATH

Figure 1

3. What is the travel time from A to B along the path NENE? _____

4. List the five remaining paths and travel times from A to B using just EAST and NORTH steps.

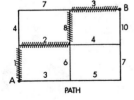

Figure 2

_____   _____

_____   _____

_____   _____

_____   _____

_____   _____

_____   _____

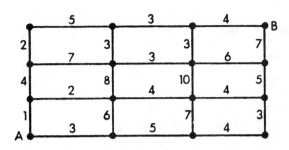

Figure 3

5. Which path took the least time? _____

6. How many minutes did it take? _____

7. How many EAST steps are in each path? _____

8. How many NORTH steps are in each path? _____

9. How many additions are required for each path? _____

Suppose we have a similar problem but with more streets involved as pictured in Figure 3.

10. Fifteen paths and travel times are given. List the 5 remaining paths and travel times, remembering that at each corner you must go EAST or NORTH.

Paths	Travel Times (Minutes)
EEENNN	27
EENENN	31
EENNEN	38
EENNNE	32
ENEENN	29
ENENEN	36
ENENNE	30
NEEENN	23
NEENEN	30
NEENNE	24
NNNEEE	19
NNENEE	22
NNEENE	22
NNEEEN	28
NENNEE	21
_____	_____
_____	_____
_____	_____
_____	_____
_____	_____

11. Which path required the least time of travel? _____

12. How many steps are in each path? _____

13. How many EAST steps are in each path? _____

14. How many NORTH steps are in each path? _____

15. How many additions are required to find the time for each path? _____

16. How many additions are required to find the time for all paths? _____

17. Approximately how many minutes do you think it would take for you to find the travel times for all paths? _____

Again suppose we have a similar problem but with many more streets involved as pictured in Figure 4 (a 10×10 block section of the city).

18. How many steps are in each path? _____

19. How many EAST steps are in each path? _____

20. How many NORTH steps are in each path? _____

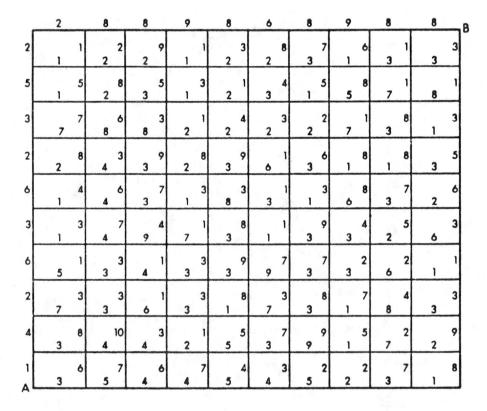

Figure 4

21. List any 5 paths and the travel times for each.

    _____   _____

    _____   _____

    _____   _____

    _____   _____

    _____   _____

22. How many additions are needed to find the travel time for each path? _____

23. Guess the total number of paths.[1] _____

24. How many additions are required to find the least travel time?

_____

25. How long would it take a computer doing 100,000 additions per second to find the answer? _____

Finally, consider a similar problem with 30 EAST and 30 NORTH steps in each path.

26. How many additions are needed to find the travel time for each path?

_____

27. Calculate the number of paths. _____

28. Approximately how many additions are required to find the least travel time?

_____

29. How long would it take a computer doing 100,000 additions per second to find the answer? (Recall from question 2 that 100,000 additions per second leads to 3.1536×10^{18} additions per million years.) _____

If your answer to question 29 is correct, you are now aware that a computer operating at 100,000 additions per second will require more than 2 million years to solve a 30×30 block problem.[2]

You have seen that the "brute force" method of finding the time for each path and choosing the least time can overtax the modern day computer. There are many real and important problems which are larger than the 30×30 city block problem. Such a problem arises in the optimal coding of digitized photographs received from space vehicles as described in Part IV. Hence, we cannot blithely presume that the computer can solve all such problems. Efficient techniques for solving large scale problems are required. Dynamic programming (DP) is one such technique.

---

[1] If you prefer to compute the number of paths, see Appendix I.

[2] Some proposed supercomputers will be able to do 10^9 additions per second or 3.1536×10^{16} additions per year. So even these incredibly fast machines would require over 200 years to solve the 30×30 block problem.

B. Dynamic Programming (DP) Approach

The following section demonstrates the dynamic programming (DP) solution to this shortest path problem. As you shall see, the DP approach will require at most two additions at each intersection. Since there are less than 1,000 intersections in the "30 × 30 block problem," the DP solution will require fewer than 2,000 additions. Using a computer, 2,000 additions require only a fraction of a second.

To illustrate the DP approach let us return to the 2 × 2 block case (see Figure 1). Note: We have labeled the corners with letters.

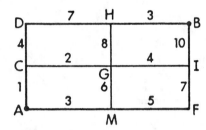

Figure 1

If we knew the least travel times from C to B and from M to B, then obviously the least travel time from A to B would be the smaller of the following two quantities:

Quantity 1:

(travel time from A to C)

+ (*least* travel time from C to B).

Quantity 2:

(travel time from A to M)

+ (*least* travel time from M to B).

Unfortunately, we do not know, in advance, the least travel time from C to B and M to B.

Similarly, if we knew the least travel times from F to B and G to B, it would be easy to compute the best path from M. But once again, we do not know (until we compute them) the least travel times from F to B and G to B.

This reasoning suggests that we work backwards from B, again with the restriction that we must always travel either NORTH or EAST. If we are at corner H, we have no choice but to go EAST which will require 3 minutes. If we are at corner I, we have no choice but to go NORTH which will require 10 minutes. Similarly from corner F we must go NORTH which will require 17 minutes to reach B. From corner D we must go EAST and in 10 minutes we reach B. We indicate these results in Figure 2, the times by the numbers in circles and the paths by the arrows.

From G we could go EAST or NORTH. Going EAST takes 4 minutes to I plus 10 minutes from I to B for a total of 14 minutes. Going NORTH from G takes 8 minutes to H plus 3 minutes from H to B for a total of 11 minutes. Thus the least time of travel from G to B is 11 minutes. We indicate this result and all previous results in Figure 3.

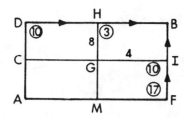

Figure 2

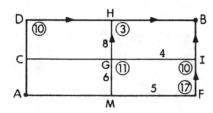

Figure 3

Going NORTH from *M* takes 6 minutes to *G* and 11 minutes from *G* to *B* using the best path. This is a total of 17 minutes. Traveling EAST from *M* takes 5 minutes to *F* and 17 minutes from *F* to *B* for a total of 22 minutes. Thus, the best path from *M* to *B* takes 17 minutes and starts in the direction NORTH from *M*. All of our results so far are illustrated in Figure 4.

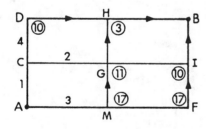

Figure 4

30. Find the best path from *C* to *B*. Should you leave corner *C* in an eastern or northern direction? _____

31. What is the least travel time from *C* to *B*? _____

32. List the best path from *A* to *B*, and tell how many minutes it requires?

_____

33. Does this answer agree with the result we obtained before? (See question 5.) _____

34. Use DP to solve the 2×3 block diagram problem in Figure 5. Time yourself.

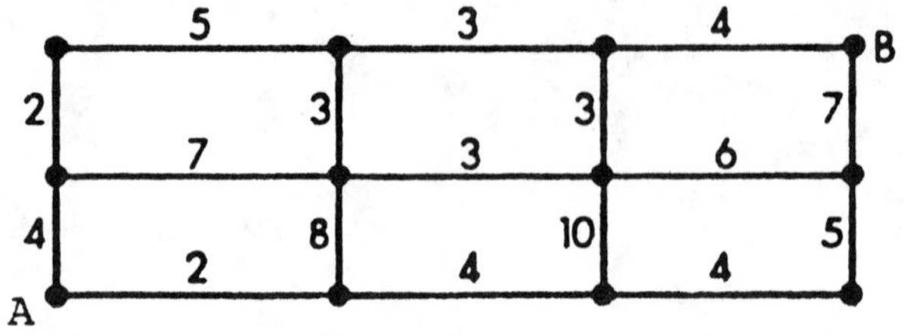

Figure 5

The optimal path is _____

Consider a 4×4 block case of our path problem. There are $8!/4!4! = 70$ paths.[1] The figure and its paths are listed in Figure 6.

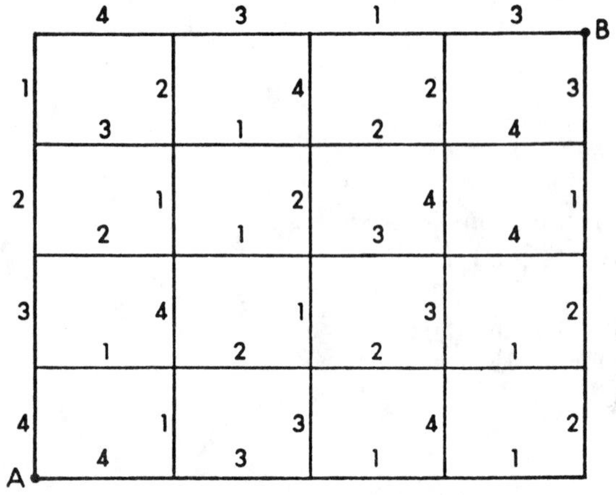

1. NNNNEEEE	19. EEENENNN	37. NNEENEEN	55. ENNENEEN
2. NNNENEEE	20. EENEENNN	38. NNEEENNE	56. ENNEENNE
3. NNNEENEE	21. ENEEENNN	39. NNEEEEN	57. ENNEENEN
4. NNNEEENE	22. NEEEENNN	40. NNEEEENN	58. ENNEEENN
5. NNNEEEEN	23. EEENNENN	41. NENENNEE	59. ENENNNEE
6. NNENNEEE	24. EENENENN	42. NENENENE	60. ENENNENE
7. NNENENEE	25. ENEENENN	43. NENENEEN	61. ENENNEEN
8. NNENEENE	26. NEEENENN	44. NENEENNE	62. ENENENNE
9. NNENEEEN	27. EEENNNEN	45. NENEENEN	63. ENENENEN
10. NENNNEEE	28. EENENNEN	46. NENEEENN	64. ENENEENN
11. NENNENEE	29. ENEENNEN	47. NEENNNEE	65. EENNNNEE
12. NENNEENE	30. NEEENNEN	48. NEENNENE	66. EENNNENE
13. NENNEEEN	31. EEENNNNE	49. NEENNEEN	67. EENNNEEN
14. ENNNEEEE	32. EENENNNE	50. NEENENNE	68. EENNENNE
15. ENNNENEE	33. ENEENNNE	51. NEENENEN	69. EENNENEN
16. ENNNEENE	34. NEEENNNE	52. NEENEENN	70. EENNEENN
17. ENNNEEEN	35. NNEENNEE	53. ENNENNEE	
18. EEEENNNN	36. NNEENENE	54. ENNENENE	

Figure 6

35. Using DP, the optimal path is _____

---

[1] See Appendix I for the meaning of the notation $8!/4!4!$.

If you are feeling ambitious, use DP to solve the 10×10 diagram problem. You should be able to do it in less than one hour. (The least travel time from A to B is 47 minutes. There are several optimal paths, one of which is: NEEEENNNEENENEEENNNN.)

Thus we see that DP is a method for quickly solving the shortest path problem. For example, Table 1 compares the numbers of additions required by the "brute force" direct enumeration and DP methods of solution for problems of varying sizes.

Table 1

Problem	Number of Additions Using Direct Enumeration	Number of Additions Using Dynamic Programming
3×3 Diagram	100	22
10×10 Diagram	3,510,364	218
30×30 Diagram	6.9797×10^{18}	1858^2

Since most computers can do at least 100,000 additions per second, the 30×30 diagram problem can be solved using the DP approach in a computer in a split second (less than 1 second). This represents a fantastic reduction from the over 2 million years of computer time required using direct enumeration.

C. How Dynamic Programming Reduces the Work Required to Solve the Shortest Path Problem

Now let's examine why the advantages of DP over the "brute force" approach are so startling.

For the 4×4 block in problem 35 there were $8!/4!4! = 70$ paths. The figure and its paths are again listed in Figure 1.

1 NNNNEEEE	19. EEEENENNN	37. NNEEENEEN	55. ENNENEEN
2. NNNENEEE	20. EENEEENNN	38. NNEEEENNE	56. ENNEENNE
3. NNNEENEE	21. ENEEEENNN	39. NNEEEENEN	57. ENNEENEN
4. NNNEEENE	22. NEEEEENNN	40. NNEEEEENN	58. ENNEEENN
5. NNNEEEEN	23. EEENNENN	41. NENENNEE	59. ENENNNEE
6. NNENNEEE	24. EEENENEN	42. NENENENE	60. ENENNENE
7. NNENENEE	25. ENEEENENN	43. NENENEEN	61. ENENNEEN
8. NNENEENE	26. NEEEENENN	44. NENEENNE	62. ENENENNE
9. NNENEEEN	27. EEENNNEN	45. NENEENEN	63. ENENENEN
10. NENNNEEE	28. EENENNEN	46. NENEEENN	64. ENENEENN
11. NENNENEE	29. ENEENNEN	47. NENNNEE	65. EENNNNEE
12. NENNEENE	30. NEEENNEN	48. NENNNENE	66. EENNNENE
13. NENNEEEN	31. EEENNNNE	49. NENNEEN	67. EENNNEEN
14. ENNNNEEE	32. EENENNNE	50. NEENENNE	68. EENNENNE
15. ENNNENEE	33. ENEENNNE	51. NEENENEN	69. EENNENEN
16. ENNNEENE	34. NEEENNNE	52. NEENEENN	70. EENNEENN
17. ENNNEEEN	35. NNEENNEE	53. ENNENNEE	
18. EEEENNNN	36. NNEENENE	54. ENNENENE	

Figure 1

---

[2] The number 1858 is obtained in the following way: A 30×30 diagram has $31 \times 31 = 961$ intersections. For 58 of the 961 intersections on North or East boundaries, only one addition is required. For 3 intersections on those boundaries, no addition is required (which ones?). For each of the remaining 900 intersections, 2 additions are required.

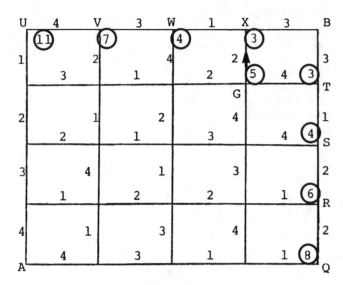

Figure 2

Find the shortest path solution to this 4 × 4 block problem using DP. However, this time as you compute the minimum time to reach B from each corner, strike from the list of all paths those that could not possibly be the optimal path from A to B. For example, suppose you have proceeded to the stage of calculations indicated in Figure 2. The results at corners U, V, W, X, T, S, R, and Q do not allow you to rule out any paths as the candidates for the best path from A to B, since paths which reach any of these "edge points" can proceed only in one direction. However, the result at corner G enables you to rule out any path which takes you to G and then proceeds EAST. The 5 and northern pointing arrow (↑) at G indicate that regardless of how you get to G, you will minimize the remaining travel time by going NORTH from G. Therefore, any path which ends in EN cannot possibly be the shortest time path from A to B (since all of these would go through G, having 3 E's and 3 N's in the first six steps, and then proceed EAST). There are twenty paths ending with EN; these may be stricken from your list and need not be evaluated.

36. What do the paths which take you to G have in common? _____

_____

37. How many paths starting from A are there which pass through G? _____

Is it becoming apparent why DP is efficient? As stated previously, as soon as you determine that NORTH is the best step from Corner G you are immediately able to eliminate 20 paths from consideration as optimal paths from A to B, without really having to compute the times associated with them. Using the "brute force" method, however, you are not able to eliminate any path from consideration.

Continue to compute the best path from each corner. After each computation strike from the list of 70 possible paths those that cannot be optimal.

To this point you have seen DP applied to the shortest path problem and should now have some appreciation for its efficiency.

D. **Mathematical Formulation of the DP Approach and the Principle of Optimality**

Let us now consider the mathematical formulation of the DP approach and its theoretical foundation, the *principle of optimality*. This formalism will enable you to apply the technique to other problems.

Let us return again to the 2×2 diagram. This time a coordinate system has been introduced (see Figure 1), and you will express the dynamic programming approach to the shortest path problem using mathematical terms.

Let (x, y) represent an intersection or corner in the diagram. For example, $(1,1)$ is the corner of Oak and Ash and the point A is located at the origin $(0,0)$. Now let $f(x, y)$ represent the least time of travel from (x, y) to B. So $f(x, y)$ is the notation for the circled numbers used previously. For example, $f(1, 1) = 11$ is the shortest time from the corner of Oak and Ash to B.

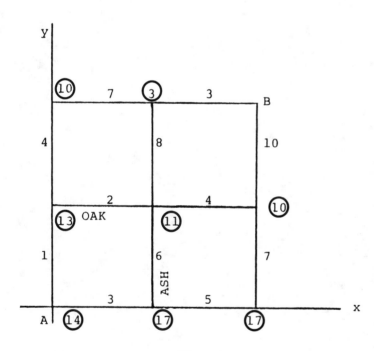

Figure 1

38. What is $f(1, 0)$? _____

39. What is $f(0, 1)$? _____

Proceeding with your mathematical representation, let $t_E(x, y)$ be the time required to go EAST from corner (x, y) to corner $(x + 1, y)$. Let $t_N(x, y)$ be the time required to go NORTH from corner (x, y) to corner $(x, y + 1)$; see Figure 2.

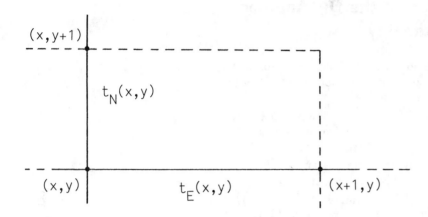

Figure 2

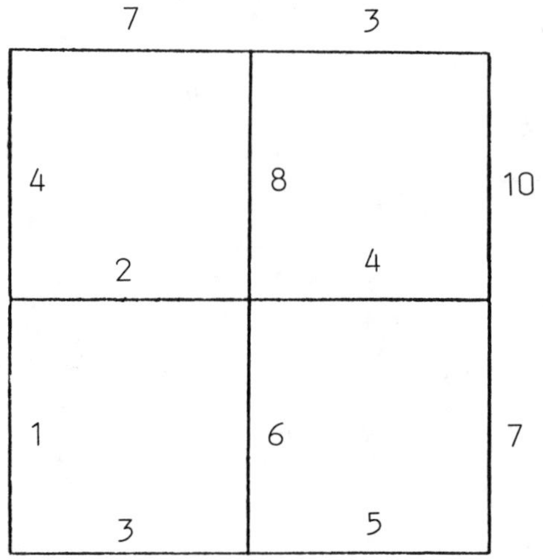

Figure 3

For example, in Figure 3 $t_E(1,1) = 4$ and $t_N(1,1) = 8$.
What are the following times:

40. $t_N(0,0)$? _____

41. $t_N(1,0)$? _____

42. $t_N(2,1)$? _____

Now, when working backwards to assign a circled number at a point (x,y), the appropriate numbers, $f(x+1,y)$ and $f(x,y+1)$, must already be circled at $(x+1,y)$ and $(x,y+1)$; see Figure 4.

Using this notation for the DP approach to the problem, one observes that $f(x,y)$ is either

$$t_E(x,y) + f(x+1,y) \quad \text{or} \quad t_N(x,y) + f(x,y+1),$$

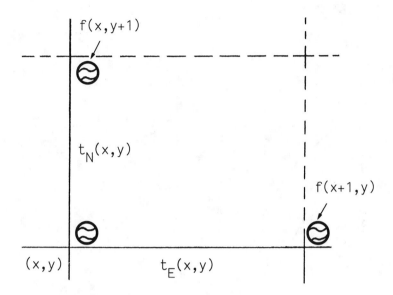

Figure 4

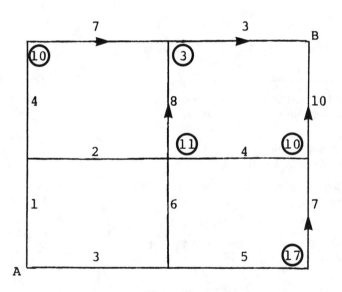

Figure 5

whichever is smaller. A more concise representation is:

(1) $f(x, y) = \text{minimum}[t_E(x, y) + f(x + 1, y); t_N(x, y) + f(x, y + 1)]$.

For example, in Figure 5

$$f(0, 1) = \text{minimum}[t_E(0, 1) + f(1, 1); t_N(0, 1) + f(0, 2)]$$
$$= \text{minimum}[13, 14] = 13.$$

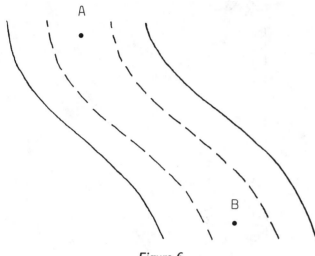

Figure 6

Fill in the missing values needed to complete the following:

43.
$$f(1,0) = \text{minimum}[t_E(\quad,\quad) + f(\quad,\quad); t_N(\quad,\quad) + f(\quad,\quad)]$$
$$= \text{minimum}[\quad,\quad] = \underline{\hspace{3cm}}.$$

44.
$$f(0,0) = \text{minimum}[t_E(\quad,\quad) + f(\quad,\quad); t_N(\quad,\quad) + f(\quad,\quad)]$$
$$= \text{minimum}[\quad,\quad] = \underline{\hspace{3cm}}.$$

Equation (1) is called a *functional equation* and is used to solve a *shortest path problem*. As you continue to study dynamic programming, you will see other examples of functional equations.

Equation (1) can be used to introduce the principle of optimality, which is the cornerstone of dynamic programming. The principle states that:

> *An optimal (best) policy has the property that whatever the initial "state" and first "decision" are, the remaining decisions must be an optimal policy with regard to the state resulting from the first decision.*

This may seem to be a silly statement, because almost everyone realizes that, for an optimal policy, the *first* decision and all remaining decisions are optimal.

The principle of optimality gives special emphasis to the first decision and therein lies the secret of its effectiveness.

By distinguishing between the first decision and all others, you can write a functional equation that provides a computational solution to the problem.

There is a geometric interpretation of the principle of optimality. Consider a surface with two points *A* and *B* as illustrated in Figure 6. Suppose the shortest path from *A* to *B* on this surface is path *p* shown in Figure 7. Suppose point *C* is the state (location) resulting from the first decision, as in Figure 8. The possible paths from *C* to *B* represent "remaining decisions" once *C* is reached.

It should be clear that the shortest path from *C* to *B* is along path *p*. For suppose there is another path from *C* to *B*, say *p'* (*p'* is represented by the

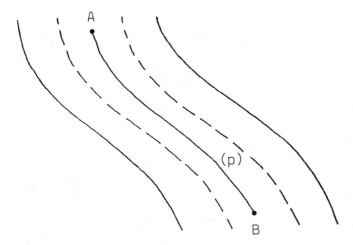

Figure 7

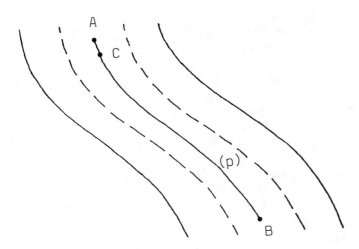

Figure 8

dotted line in Figure 9), which is shorter. Then the path from *A* to *B* where one follows path *p* from *A* to *C* and then proceeds to *B* by way of *p'* would be a shorter path from *A* to *B* than *p*. Thus *p* could not be the shortest path from *A* to *B*.

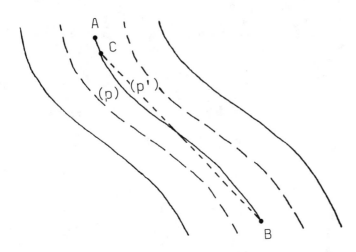

Figure 9

Let's examine this principle in terms of our shortest path block problem. A policy is simply the choice of a path, i.e., a sequence of N's and E's that leads from A to B. An optimal policy is that path from A to B which requires the least time. The initial state is that you are located at A. Your original decision is the selection of the direction NORTH or EAST for the first leg of your journey. Once you have made your initial decision, arbitrary though it may be, you want to do the best you can (in terms of travel time) with your remaining choices.

But recall that $f(x, y)$ stands for the least time from (x, y) to B, and so you do not have the luxury of an arbitrary first choice and optimal remaining choices given that first choice. You remove this arbitrariness by comparing the travel time of each possible first choice taken together with the optimum time for the remaining steps given that first choice. You then choose the alternative with the least total time of travel. For the shortest path problem where there are only two possible first choices, NORTH and EAST, the words above were expressed mathematically in equation (1) which is rewritten below:

$$f(x, y) = \text{minimum}[t_E(x, y) + f(x + 1, y); t_N(x, y) + f(x, y + 1)].$$

Hence, in applying this equation while working backwards from B to A, when you arrive at A and evaluate $f(0, 0)$, the principle of optimality assures you of finding the shortest time (and path) from A to B.

Richard Bellman,[1] the "father" of DP, has stated that the principle of optimality is a simple but elusive concept, which requires a great deal of practice to master.

If you have completed and understand the material presented so far, you have progressed admirably toward understanding dynamic programming. The material which follows applies dynamic programming to problems that arise in government, industry, and science.

The shrub cover problem, presented next, may seem unrealistic. However, it is a disguise for an actual military problem with security classification.

---

[1] For a short biography of Richard Bellman, see Appendix II.

Part II
A SHRUB COVERING (ASSORTMENT) PROBLEM

Suppose you are a homeowner wanting to protect ten different-sized shrubs from frost. It seems that the best way to cover them is to buy ten different-sized covers, each tailored to a particular shrub.

Several department stores are contacted, and none has such covers. However, one store offers to manufacture covers for you, but in at most three sizes. Any given cover size will also cover a shrub requiring a smaller size. For example, a size 7 cover will also cover shrubs with smaller sizes 6, 5, 4, 3, 2, 1. The store provides the prices for the ten sizes as given in Table 1. Once you have chosen the three sizes to be manufactured, you may purchase as many as you wish of each size. Your objective is to select the three sizes which enable you to cover all shrubs at least cost.

Table 1

Cover Size Number i	Cost (in dollars) C_i
1	$C_1 = 1$
2	$C_2 = 4$
3	$C_3 = 5$
4	$C_4 = 7$
5	$C_5 = 8$
6	$C_6 = 12$
7	$C_7 = 13$
8	$C_8 = 18$
9	$C_9 = 19$
10	$C_{10} = 21$

45. Could it be less costly to choose fewer than the three sizes you are allowed? Why or why not?

_____

_____

_____

It is clear that you will need size 10 for the largest shrub. So, actually, you have to select only two other sizes. Suppose you choose sizes 10, 5, and 3. Size 10 covers will be used to cover shrubs 10, 9, 8, 7, and 6; size 5 covers will be used to cover shrubs 5 and 4; and size 3 covers will be used to cover shrubs 3, 2, and 1.

We call any choice of three sizes a policy. Your goal is to find a policy which results in least cost.

46. (a) Using the cost data, find the cost for the policy consisting of sizes 10, 5, and 3. _____

You could solve this problem by your old stand-by "brute-force" method, sometimes called the exhaustive search technique. That is, you could find the costs for all policies (all possible combinations of three cover sizes) and select the policy with the smallest cost. Since cover size 10 is included in every combination, there are $\binom{9}{2} = 36$ policies because there are 36 ways to choose two sizes from nine.[1] Table 2 gives 30 of the 36 policies and their costs.

46. (b) Fill in the remaining 6 policies and their costs in the spaces provided.

Table 2
Cost Data

Cover size i	1	2	3	4	5	6	7	8	9	10
Cost C_i	1	4	5	7	8	12	13	18	19	21

	Combination of Sizes	Cost of Policy		Combination of Sizes	Cost of Policy
1	10,9,8	$184	19	10,7,3	$130
2	10,9,7	150	20	10,7,2	136
3	10,9,6	150	21	10,7,1	142
4	10,9,5	137	22	10,6,5	136
5	10,9,4	144	23	10,6,4	136
6	10,9,3	150	24	10,6,3	135
7	10,9,2	162	25	10,6,2	140
8	10,9,1	174	26	10,6,1	145
9	10,8,7	151	27	10,5,4	141
10	10,8,6	148	28	10,5,3	136
11	10,8,5	136	29	10,5,2	137
12	10,8,4	142	30	10,5,1	138
13	10,8,3	147	31	_____	_____
14	10,8,2	158	32	_____	_____
15	10,8,1	169	33	_____	_____
16	10,7,6	148	34	_____	_____
17	10,7,5	129	35	_____	_____
18	10,7,4	130	36	_____	_____

[1] See Appendix I.

47. Which policy has the smallest cost? _____

48. Is there more than one policy which has the smallest cost? _____

Because the sample problem is small, the exhaustive search technique provided a solution in reasonable time. However, for larger problems determined by the number of shrubs and the number of allowable cover sizes, the exhaustive search method is exhausting, even for a computer. For example, if the problem were to select 31 sizes to cover 61 shrubs, the number of combinations for consideration using exhaustive search would be $C(60, 30)$, the number of combinations of 60 things taken 30 at a time. (And you know how big that is!) A computer that does 100,000 additions per second would require more than two million years to solve the problem by exhaustive search. The same problem can be solved in less than one minute using dynamic programming and a computer. Let's move on to the dynamic programming solution.

Let us restate the principle of optimality which will be your guide in formulating the dynamic programming solution.

An optimal policy has the property that whatever the initial 'state' and initial 'decision' are, the remaining decisions must be an optimal policy with regard to the state resulting from the first decision.

For the general shrub covering problem, you are to choose k cover sizes for x shrubs $(k \leq x)$. A policy is a combination of k cover sizes . An optimal policy is a combination of k cover sizes that gives the least cost. The initial state is x, which means you are intending to cover shrubs $1, 2, \ldots, x$; and the initial decision is the selection of the next largest cover size, y, that you will choose in addition to x, the size needed to cover the largest shrub.

Once you have chosen y, arbitrary though the choice may be, you will want to do the best you can with respect to the remaining $k - 2$ choices.

Recall that in the shortest path problem, you defined a function $f(x, y)$ as:

$f(x, y) = $ the least time of travel from the point (x, y) to B.

You worked your way backwards from B to A, whose coordinates were $(0, 0)$. $f(0, 0)$ represented the time of the shortest path from A to B. You will use a similar strategy to define the shrub-cover problem.

Let the function $f_k(x)$ be the least cost of covering shrubs $1, 2, \ldots, x$ using k covers of different sizes. With this notation $f_3(10)$ is interpreted as the least cost of covering plants $1, 2, \ldots, 10$ with 3 different-sized covers.

What is the meaning of:

49. $f_1(1)$? _____

50. $f_1(3)$? _____

51. $f_2(5)$? _____

52. Does $f_2(1)$ make sense? _____

53. Does $f_3(7)$ make sense? _____

Applying the principle of optimality, let us write an expression with our newly defined function, which gives the cost associated with a policy composed of size x, an arbitrarily chosen size y, and the best choices for the remaining $k - 2$ sizes:[1]

$$(x - y)C_x + f_{k-1}(y)$$
1st term   2nd term

The first term in the expression gives the cost of covering shrubs, $x, x - 1, \ldots,$ $y + 1$, of which there are $(x - y)$, with the largest cover size x. The second term gives, by definition, the least cost of covering bushes $1, 2, \ldots, y$ with $k - 1$ cover sizes, which includes size y.

But the symbol $f_k(x)$ calls for all choices to be optimal, not one arbitrary and the remaining optimal given that choice. Recall that in the shortest path problem you resolved this dilemma by letting the initial choice vary over all the alternatives and then choosing the minimum total cost. Using the same approach here, you can write an expression for $f_k(x)$ that eliminates the arbitrariness:

(2) $$f_k(x) = \underset{\{y\}}{\text{minimum}} \{(x - y)C_x + f_{k-1}(y)\}.$$

Equation (2) is a functional equation that evolves from the principle of optimality. The notation on the right-hand side of equation (2) means that you are to evaluate the expression inside the bracket for all possible values of y, then choose the minimum (smallest) value among them. For example,

$$f_2(4) = \underset{\{y\}}{\text{minimum}} \{(4 - y)C_4 + f_1(y)\}.$$

There are 3 possible choices for y; y could be 3, 2, or 1. Hence $f_2(4)$ is the smallest of 3 values $C_4 + f_1(3)$ OR $2C_4 + f_1(2)$ OR $3C_4 + f_1(1)$.

For your specific problem, you want to determine $f_3(10)$. You see from equation (2):

$$f_3(10) = \underset{\{y\}}{\text{minimum}} \{(10 - y)C_{10} + f_2(y)\},$$

where y varies over the set $\{9, 8, \ldots, 2\}$.

To compute $f_3(10)$ you need to know $f_2(y)$ for different values of y. But it is apparent, again from equation (2), that $f_2(y)$ for a particular value of y, say $y = 9$, requires the function $f_1(y)$. In fact:

$$f_2(9) = \underset{\{z\}}{\text{minimum}} \{(9 - z)C_9 + f_1(z)\},$$

where z varies over the set $\{8, 7, \ldots, 1\}$. So it will be necessary to compute $f_1(x)$ first, then $f_2(x)$, and finally $f_3(10)$. By definition, $f_1(1)$ means the least cost of covering the smallest shrub with one cover. This is achieved by covering the smallest shrub with the cover tailored for it.

54. What is the value of $f_1(1)$? _____

To find the value of $f_1(2)$, the least cost of covering the smallest two shrubs with one size cover, we will have to use two size 2 covers at a cost of $8. So $f_1(2) = 8$.

---

[1] It helps the reader here to have a concrete case in mind, such as $x = 10, k = 5, y = 7$.

Similarly, we build up the following table:

$$f_1(1) = C_1 = 1 \cdot 1 = 1$$
$$f_1(2) = 2C_2 = 2 \cdot 4 = 8$$
$$f_1(3) = 3C_3 = 3 \cdot 5 = 15$$
$$f_1(4) = 4C_4 = 4 \cdot 7 = 28$$
$$f_1(5) = 5C_5 = 5 \cdot 8 = 40$$
$$f_1(6) = 6C_6 = 6 \cdot 12 = 72$$
$$f_1(7) = 7C_7 = 7 \cdot 13 = 91$$
$$f_1(8) = 8C_8 = 8 \cdot 18 = 144$$
$$f_1(9) = 9C_9 = 9 \cdot 19 = 171$$
$$f_1(10) = 10C_{10} = 10 \cdot 21 = 210$$

To compute $f_2(x)$, you use equation (2) with $k = 2$. That is,

$$f_2(x) = \underset{\{y\}}{\text{minimum}} \{(x - y)C_x + f_1(y)\}.$$

The results are given below for $x = 2, 3, \ldots, 9$. You can stop here with $x = 9$ since $f_2(10)$ is not required to compute $f_3(10)$.

$f_2(2) = C_1 + C_2 = 5$

$f_2(3) = $ minimum of $\left\{ \begin{array}{l} C_3 + f_1(2) = 5 + 8 = 13 \\ 2C_3 + f_1(1) = 10 + 1 = 11 \end{array} \right\} = 2C_3 + f_1(1) = 11$

$f_2(4) = $ minimum of $\left\{ \begin{array}{l} C_4 + f_1(3) = 7 + 15 = 22 \\ 2C_4 + f_1(2) = 14 + 8 = 22 \\ 3C_4 + f_1(1) = 21 + 1 = 22 \end{array} \right\} = 22$

$f_2(5) = $ minimum of $\left\{ \begin{array}{l} C_5 + f_1(4) = 8 + 28 = 36 \\ 2C_5 + f_1(3) = 16 + 15 = 31 \\ 3C_5 + f_1(2) = 24 + 8 = 32 \\ 4C_5 + f_1(1) = 32 + 1 = 33 \end{array} \right\} = 2C_5 + f_1(3) = 31$

$f_2(6) = $ minimum of $\left\{ \begin{array}{l} C_6 + f_1(5) = 12 + 40 = 52 \\ 2C_6 + f_1(4) = 24 + 28 = 52 \\ 3C_6 + f_1(3) = 36 + 15 = 51 \\ 4C_6 + f_1(2) = 48 + 8 = 56 \\ 5C_6 + f_1(1) = 60 + 1 = 61 \end{array} \right\} = 3C_6 + f_1(3) = 51$

$f_2(7) = $ minimum of $\left\{ \begin{array}{l} C_7 + f_1(6) = 13 + 72 = 85 \\ 2C_7 + f_1(5) = 26 + 40 = 66 \\ 3C_7 + f_1(4) = 39 + 28 = 67 \\ 4C_7 + f_1(3) = 52 + 15 = 67 \\ 5C_7 + f_1(2) = 65 + 8 = 73 \\ 6C_7 + f_1(1) = 78 + 1 = 79 \end{array} \right\} = 2C_7 + f_1(5) = 66$

$$f_2(8) = \text{minimum of} \left\{ \begin{array}{l} C_8 + f_1(7) = 18 + 91 = 109 \\ 2C_8 + f_1(6) = 36 + 72 = 108 \\ 3C_8 + f_1(5) = 54 + 40 = 94 \\ 4C_8 + f_1(4) = 72 + 28 = 100 \\ 5C_8 + f_1(3) = 90 + 15 = 105 \\ 6C_8 + f_1(2) = 108 + 8 = 116 \\ 7C_8 + f_1(1) = 124 + 1 = 125 \end{array} \right\} = 3C_8 + f_1(5) = 94$$

$$f_2(9) = \text{minimum of} \left\{ \begin{array}{l} C_9 + f_1(8) = 19 + 144 = 163 \\ 2C_9 + f_1(7) = 38 + 91 = 129 \\ 3C_9 + f_1(6) = 57 + 72 = 129 \\ 4C_9 + f_1(5) = 76 + 40 = 116 \\ 5C_9 + f_1(4) = 95 + 28 = 123 \\ 6C_9 + f_1(3) = 114 + 15 = 129 \\ 7C_9 + f_1(2) = 133 + 8 = 141 \\ 8C_9 + f_1(1) = 152 + 1 = 153 \end{array} \right\} = 4C_9 + f_1(5) = 116.$$

Finally, we compute $f_3(10)$. Again from equation (2) we have:

$$f_3(10) = \underset{\{y\}}{\text{minimum}} \{(10 - y)C_{10} + f_2(y)\}.$$

Therefore:

$$f_3(10) = \text{minimum of} \left\{ \begin{array}{l} C_{10} + f_2(9) = 21 + 116 = 137 \\ 2C_{10} + f_2(8) = 42 + 94 = 136 \\ 3C_{10} + f_2(7) = 63 + 66 = 129 \\ 4C_{10} + f_2(6) = 84 + 51 = 135 \\ 5C_{10} + f_2(5) = 105 + 31 = 136 \\ 6C_{10} + f_2(4) = 126 + 22 = 148 \\ 7C_{10} + f_2(3) = 147 + 11 = 158 \\ 8C_{10} + f_2(2) = 168 + 5 = 173 \end{array} \right\} = 3C_{10} + f_2(7) = 129.$$

From $f_3(10)$ you see that your optimal solution uses 3 covers of size 10. That is,

$$f_3(10) = 3C_{10} + f_2(7) = 129.$$

Recall that $f_2(7) = 2C_7 + f_1(5)$. Hence

$$f_3(10) = 3C_{10} + 2C_7 + f_1(5).$$

From this expression you can see that the least cost is obtained by covering bushes 10, 9, 8 with cover size 10, covering bushes 7 and 6 with cover size 7, and covering the five remaining bushes with cover size 5. The best policy (10, 7, 5), of course, agrees with that found using exhaustive search.

For the solution of the general problem, (x shrubs, k sizes), by dynamic programming, the number of computer operations (additions, multiplications, table look-ups, and comparisons) required is less than $2kx(x+1)$. For $k = 30$ and $x = 60$, $2kx(x+1) = 220,000$. Current computers could find the solution in less than a minute. Recall that the exhaustive search procedure required more than two million years by computer.

55. Use equation (2) and the results generated so far to compute $f_4(10)$.

$$f_4(10) = \underline{\hspace{5cm}}$$

Part III
ADDITIONAL ASSORTMENT PROBLEMS

The shrub cover problem is one of a class of assortment problems. In fact there are an "assortment of assortment" problems which arise frequently in practice: the sizing of military helmets, the sizing of steel beams, and the selection of gray levels for transmission of digitized photographs from space vehicles are a few examples.

In this section we describe several of these problems. You will be given the opportunity to formulate them as dynamic programming problems.

A. Helmet Sizing Problem

Suppose you are given a major task of selecting sizes in which a new army helmet will be produced. Because too many sizes cause production, storage, and distribution problems, you are told not to exceed 3 sizes. You begin by defining a helmet "size" as hat size. To collect data regarding hat sizes, you select 10,000 soldiers at random and record their hat sizes. In your sample you find that all of the hat sizes fall between size 6 and size 8. You determine the fraction of the 10,000 soldiers with each hat size as shown in Table 1.

Table 1

Hat Size i	6	$6\frac{1}{8}$	$6\frac{1}{4}$	$6\frac{3}{8}$	$6\frac{1}{2}$	$6\frac{5}{8}$	$6\frac{3}{4}$	$6\frac{7}{8}$	7	$7\frac{1}{8}$	$7\frac{1}{4}$	$7\frac{3}{8}$	$7\frac{1}{2}$	$7\frac{5}{8}$	$7\frac{3}{4}$	$7\frac{7}{8}$	8
Fraction (F_i) Soldiers with Hat Size i	0.02	0.01	0.03	0.05	0.05	0.06	0.07	0.07	0.11	0.10	0.11	0.09	0.06	0.08	0.05	0.03	0.01

To fit all soldiers, size 8 must be one of the sizes selected. Your responsibility is to find two other sizes that, together with size 8, constitute the best choice. Candidates for your choice are sizes 8, $7\frac{7}{8}$, $7\frac{3}{4}$, or sizes 8, $7\frac{7}{8}$, $7\frac{5}{8}$, or any other of the 120 combinations[1] of three sizes that include size 8.

If a soldier with hat size 7 is fitted with size $7\frac{1}{2}$, the oversize is $\frac{1}{2}$. In general if a soldier with hat size x is fitted with y (clearly $y \geq x$), the oversize is $y - x$.

---

[1]Size 8 is included in every combination. There are sixteen other sizes from which two are to be selected. Hence there are $C(16, 2) = 16!/2!14! = 120$ possible combinations.

Table 2

	Hat size i	Fraction of Soldiers F_i	The oversizing by hat size for the choice of helmet sizes $x = 7$, $y = 7\frac{1}{2}$, and $z = 8$:
1	6	0.02	$(7 - 6)$
2	$6\frac{1}{8}$	0.01	$(7 - 6\frac{1}{8})$
3	$6\frac{1}{4}$	0.03	$(7 - 6\frac{1}{4})$
4	$6\frac{3}{8}$	0.05	$(7 - 6\frac{3}{8})$
5	$6\frac{1}{2}$	0.05	$(7 - 6\frac{1}{2})$
6	$6\frac{5}{8}$	0.06	$(7 - 6\frac{5}{8})$
7	$6\frac{3}{4}$	0.07	$(7 - 6\frac{3}{4})$
8	$6\frac{7}{8}$	0.07	$(7 - 6\frac{7}{8})$
9	7	0.11	$(7 - 7)$
10	$7\frac{1}{8}$	0.10	$(7\frac{1}{2} - 7\frac{1}{8})$
11	$7\frac{1}{4}$	0.11	$(7\frac{1}{2} - 7\frac{1}{4})$
12	$7\frac{3}{8}$	0.09	$(7\frac{1}{2} - 7\frac{3}{8})$
13	$7\frac{1}{2}$	0.06	$(7\frac{1}{2} - 7\frac{1}{2})$
14	$7\frac{5}{8}$	0.08	$(8 - 7\frac{5}{8})$
15	$7\frac{3}{4}$	0.05	$(8 - 7\frac{3}{4})$
16	$7\frac{7}{8}$	0.03	$(8 - 7\frac{7}{8})$
17	8	0.01	$(8 - 8)$

Your objective for the best three sizes are those which result in the least oversizing on the average. Suppose you selected sizes 8, $7\frac{1}{2}$, and 7. Size 8 helmets would be given to any soldier whose hat size was less than or equal to 8 and greater than $7\frac{1}{2}$. Size $7\frac{1}{2}$ helmets would be issued to soldiers with hat sizes $7\frac{1}{2}$, $7\frac{3}{8}$, $7\frac{1}{4}$, or $7\frac{1}{8}$. Size 7 helmets are issued to any soldier whose hat size is less than or equal to 7.

The "average oversizing" for this selection of helmet sizes can be obtained from the data in Table 2.

The average oversizing is computed in the following way. The 2% (.02) of the soldiers with size 6 hat size are given size 7 helmets, for an oversizing of $(7 - 6) = 1$. The 1% (.01) of soldiers with size $6\frac{1}{8}$, also given size 7, have an oversize of $(7 - 6\frac{1}{8}) = \frac{7}{8}$. Over all sizes, the *average* oversizing is:

$$.02(7 - 6) + .01(7 - 6\frac{1}{8}) + .03(7 - 6\frac{1}{4}) + \cdots + .01(8 - 8),$$

which equals .27875.

56. Using a calculator, determine the "average oversizing" for the selection 8, $7\frac{1}{4}$, $6\frac{5}{8}$. _____

Generally, the oversizing function for the selection of 3 sizes $x < y < z$ may be described algebraically. Let $T(x, y, z)$ be the average oversizing for sizes x, y, z. Then $T(x, y, z) = G(x) + G_x(y) + G_y(z)$, where

$G(x)$ is the average oversizing for the soldiers fitted with x. Since x is the smallest size selected, it would be for soldiers with hat size $\leq x$.

$G_x(y)$ is the average oversizing for the soldiers fitted with y (those larger than x and not larger than y).

$G_y(z)$ is the average oversizing for all soldiers fitted with z (those larger than y and not larger than z).

In the example, with $x = 7$, $y = 7\frac{1}{2}$, and $z = 8$, you have

Table 3

	Hat size i	Frequency of hat size × oversizing	
1	6	$0.02\ (7 - 6)$	
2	$6\frac{1}{8}$	$0.01\ (7 - 6\frac{1}{8})$	
3	$6\frac{1}{4}$	$0.03\ (7 - 6\frac{1}{4})$	
4	$6\frac{3}{8}$	$0.05\ (7 - 6\frac{3}{8})$	
5	$6\frac{1}{2}$	$0.05\ (7 - 6\frac{1}{2})$	Sum is
6	$6\frac{5}{8}$	$0.06\ (7 - 6\frac{5}{8})$	$G(x) = G(7) = .15625.$
7	$6\frac{3}{4}$	$0.07\ (7 - 6\frac{3}{4})$	
8	$6\frac{7}{8}$	$0.07\ (7 - 6\frac{7}{8})$	
9	7	$0.11\ (7 - 7)$	
10	$7\frac{1}{8}$	$0.10\ (7\frac{1}{2} - 7\frac{1}{8})$	
11	$7\frac{1}{4}$	$0.11\ (7\frac{1}{2} - 7\frac{1}{4})$	Sum is
12	$7\frac{3}{8}$	$0.09\ (7\frac{1}{2} - 7\frac{3}{8})$	$G_x(y) = G_7(7\frac{1}{2}) = .07625.$
13	$7\frac{1}{2}$	$0.06\ (7\frac{1}{2} - 7\frac{1}{2})$	
14	$7\frac{5}{8}$	$0.08\ (8 - 7\frac{5}{8})$	
15	$7\frac{3}{4}$	$0.05\ (8 - 7\frac{3}{4})$	Sum is
16	$7\frac{7}{8}$	$0.03\ (8 - 7\frac{7}{8})$	$G_y(z) = G_{7\frac{1}{2}}(8) = .04625.$
17	8	$0.01\ (8 - 8)$	
(Sum)		.27875	

57. Referring to your work in Problem 56, what are $G(6\frac{5}{8})$, $G_{6\frac{5}{8}}(7\frac{1}{4})$, and $G_{7\frac{1}{4}}(8)$? _____

The four-star general who heads the Quartermaster Corps concurs with your assumption that helmet size equals hat size and your concept of minimizing average oversizing. You are told to proceed.

58. Utilizing the principle of optimality, write a functional equation which you could use to obtain the desired solution. _____

_____

_____

There is a Help Module (Help Module A on p. 35) if you get stuck with this problem. However, the similarity between this problem and the shrub cover problem should be apparent.

An approach similar in concept, but more sophisticated, was used by the U.S. Army to assist in the sizing of their new helmet. The definition of size took into account many head measurements (circumference, height, width, ...), and the dynamic programming solution was only part of the size selection criteria.

B. Optimal Sizing of Steel Beams

Way back in the "Middle Ages" (1950s) dynamic programming was used to determine the optimum variety of sizes of steel beams to produce. The beams were each 10 meters long. Each customer required a specified strength of beams. Beam strength depends on cross-sectional area. The larger the cross-sectional area, the more costly a beam is to produce. A customer must be supplied with a beam of at least the strength he wants, but he can only be charged for a beam of precisely the strength he wants. The problem is:

What beam sizes (as determined by cross-sectional area) should be produced to fill all orders at minimum average cost to the producer?

Factory limitations allow for the manufacture of at most 3 sizes. Hypothetical "beam request and cost data" for the factory are contained in Table 1.

Table 1

Beam size requested i	Fraction of total requests for beam size i	Factory cost (hundreds of dollars) of producing beam size i (C_i)
1	0.04	2
2	0.03	7
3	0.07	8
4	0.04	10
5	0.10	11
6	0.01	14
7	0.12	20
8	0.09	23
9	0.03	24
10	0.08	26
11	0.05	30
12	0.08	33
13	0.16	35
14	0.06	45
15	0.04	50

Suppose the company chose to fill all requests with beam sizes 15, 10, and 5. Size 15 is used to fill orders for sizes 15, 14, 13, 12, 11 or 0.39 of the requests. The fraction 0.39 is obtained by adding the fraction of requests for sizes 11 to 15. Size 10 is used to fill orders for the beam sizes 10, 9, 8, 7, 6 or 0.33 of the requests. Size 5 is used for the sizes 5, 4, 3, 2, 1 or 0.28 of the requests. The average cost for filling all orders is

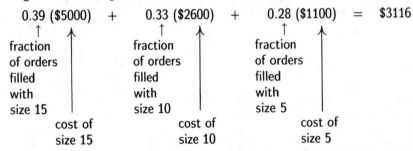

The average cost for filling all orders with sizes 15, 13, and 7 is

$$0.10(5000) + 0.49(3500) + 0.41(2000) = \$3035,$$

which is less than for the combination 15, 10, 5. The problem is to find the combination of three sizes which gives the least cost of filling all requests. Obviously size 15 must be one of the three. You could find the solution by computing the average cost for each of the ninety-one combinations (from fourteen sizes you choose two) involving size 15. Instead, try doing it by dynamic programming.

59. Using the principle of optimality, write a functional equation that could be used to obtain the least average cost solution that satisfies all requests.

There is a Help Module (Help Module B on p. 36) if you need it.

If you have completed and understand the shortest path, shrub covering, helmet sizing, and steel beam problems—YOU ARE TO BE CONGRATULATED!! REALLY! You have mastered an important part of the theory and application of DP. This material is often not taught until graduate school. If you still feel unsure, review the material and use the help modules provided.

If you're feeling *very* confident—go on to the next problem. It's quite difficult and should be attempted only when the previous material has been totally mastered. Good luck to you adventurous souls who go on!

Part IV
OPTIMAL CODING OF DIGITIZED PHOTOGRAPHS

As you may know, photographs obtained from satellites or other space vehicles can be stored or transmitted as numbers. For black and white photographs each number represents one of n gray levels (shades of gray from very white to very black). Each gray level corresponds to the intensity of light reflected from a small region of the original scene.

Such photographs are called digitized photographs. The level of detail that can be observed in the digitized version depends partly on the value of n (the larger the value of n, the better the detail). In many applications n is either 8, 16, 32, or 64. A typical "photograph" may consist of a million areas, each one represented by an integer from the set $[0, 1, \ldots, n-1]$. These integers are usually represented as binary numbers. For example if $n = 64$, then the integers 2, 7, 63 have binary representations:

$$
\begin{array}{ll}
2 & 000010 \\
7 & 000111 \\
63 & 111111
\end{array}
$$

(Students not familiar with binary representations should see Appendix III.)

One photograph may contain as many as one million areas, which, using 64 gray levels, would take 6 million bits (0's or 1's) of data to transmit. Most applications involve thousands of photographs. This presents incredible demands on the storage and transmission capabilities of a system. Thus a design engineer is always interested in techniques that reduce the information required to the least amount necessary. These bits of information are translated by the receiving computer into gray levels, which are then plotted as a picture. The amount of detail in the picture can depend on the number of gray levels, as well as the distribution of the gray levels.

Figure 1 is a high resolution photograph of Saturn in 17 gray levels. Notice the detail in the photograph.

In many instances it is necessary or convenient to reduce the number of gray levels in a picture. When this is done, some of the detail is lost. The choice of gray levels can influence the detail which can be shown.

Figure 2 is a similar picture using lower resolution. Notice the small moon near the edge of the rings at the bottom center. It will become more or less visible depending on the gray levels we use.

Figure 3 is done in 11 gray levels numbered from 0 to 10. Suppose we want to reduce that to only three levels. Which three should we choose to preserve the important details, such as the moon?

The selection of gray levels 0, 5, and 10 results in the photograph shown in Figure 4. We have "lost" the moon. It is not visible. However for gray levels 3,

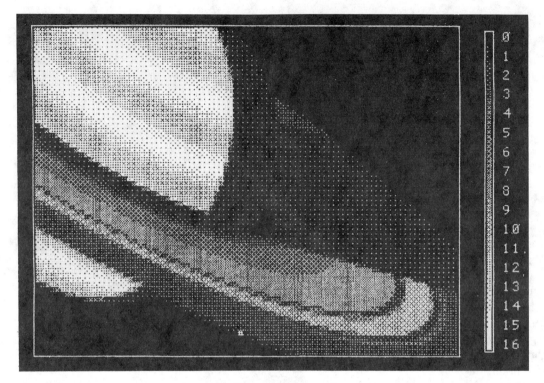

Figure 1

Figure 2

Figure 3

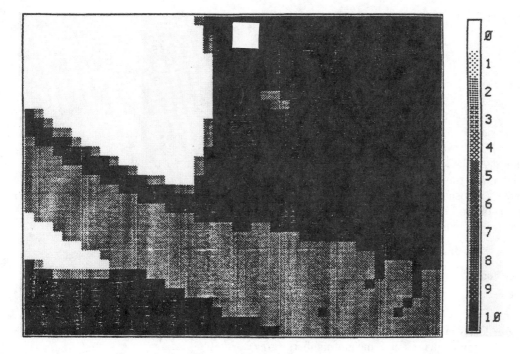

Figure 4

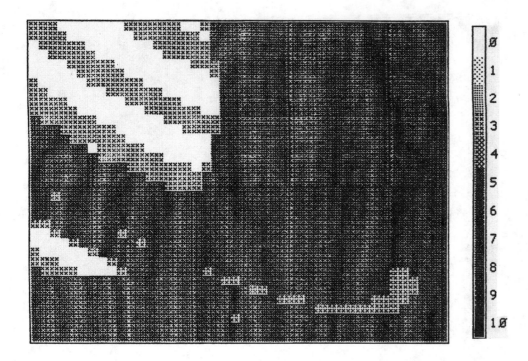

Figure 5

7, and 10, the moon is visible (see Figure 5). Clearly, the choice of gray levels is important.

Imagine the following scenario:

Digitized photographs (of Saturn) with 64 gray levels ($n = 64$) begin to arrive at the Jet Propulsion Laboratory. The scientists find these early scenes uninteresting. Until more interesting scenes appear, they would be satisfied with less detail, which could be found in a photograph using 8 gray levels. Since 8 gray levels can be represented by 3 "bit" binary numbers, we can reduce the storage and transmission requirements by 1/2. However, on the space vehicle we have the problem of converting the photographs from 64 gray levels to 8 gray levels. How would you go about selecting the 8 gray levels from among the original 64?

Several design engineers have proposed selecting the 8 gray levels which occur most frequently. Another popular criterion for selection (maybe the most popular criterion) is to minimize mean square error.

WHAT IN THE WORLD IS MEAN SQUARE ERROR?

Be patient—we intend to tell you!!

MEAN SQUARE ERROR

Let $0, 1, \ldots, 63$ be the original gray levels. Let f_i $(i = 0, 1, \ldots, 63)$ be the fraction of the total number of gray levels in the photograph that are level i.

For example, suppose the photograph consists of 1 million numbers (gray levels), 10,000 of which are level 31.

Then

$$f_{31} = \frac{10,000}{1,000,000} = 0.01$$

Suppose we select 8 gray levels, say levels 4, 11, 20, 29, 36, 45, 52, and 59. Once these are selected, each of the 64 levels is assigned to its "nearest neighbor" among the 8 selected levels, as follows:

1. Levels 0 to 7 are assigned to level 4
2. Levels 8 to 15 are assigned to level 11
3. Levels 16 to 24 are assigned to level 20
4. Levels 25 to 32 are assigned to level 29
5. Levels 33 to 40 are assigned to level 36
6. Levels 41 to 48 are assigned to level 45
7. Levels 49 to 55 are assigned to level 52
8. Levels 56 to 63 are assigned to level 59.

The mean square error for the assignment of levels 0 through 7 to level 4 is $E(4)$, where

$$E(4) = \sum_{i=0}^{7} f_i(4-i)^2$$

(Remember, f_i is the fraction of the total number of the areas in the photograph that are gray levels i.)

$$
\begin{aligned}
&= f_0(4-0)^2 + f_1(4-1)^2 + f_2(4-2)^2 + f_3(4-3)^2 \\
&\quad + f_4(4-4)^2 + f_5(4-5)^2 + f_6(4-6)^2 + f_7(4-7)^2 \\
&= 16f_0 + 9f_1 + 4f_2 + f_3 + f_5 + 4f_6 + 9f_7.
\end{aligned}
$$

Compute the mean square error for the assignments to level 11. Your answer should be

$$E(11) = 9f_8 + 4f_9 + f_{10} + f_{12} + 4f_{13} + 9f_{14} + 16f_{15}.$$

Compute $E(52)$

_____

_____

Your answer should be

$$E(52) = 9f_{49} + 4f_{50} + f_{51} + f_{53} + 4f_{54} + 9f_{55}.$$

The total mean square error, E, is defined by

$$E = E(4) + E(11) + E(20) + E(29) + E(36) + E(45) + E(52) + E(59).$$

Thus, the total mean square error is defined to be the sum of the individual mean square errors.

The problem we deal with in selecting the gray levels is to minimize the mean square error.

60. Exploit the principle of optimality to write a functional equation that could be used to select 8 gray levels that give the least total mean square error.

_____

_____

_____

Refer to Help Module C on p. 37 if you need help.

Help Modules

Help Module A. Helmet Sizing Problem

Still having trouble? Most folks do in the beginning. It takes *lots* of practice to use DP.

A good place to start is by thinking about the foundation of DP—the "principle of optimality." Remember, it says

> *An optimal policy has the property that whatever the initial state and initial decisions are, the remaining decisions must be an optimal policy with regard to the state resulting from the first decision.*

Let's apply the principle to our current problem:

A *policy* is the selection of three helmet sizes.

An *optimal policy* is a selection of sizes which minimizes the average oversizing.

The *initial state* is represented by the 17 sizes that must be assigned to 3 sizes.

The *initial decision* is the selection of the second largest size. (Remember we MUST choose the largest size in order to fit the largest head.) Our final objective is an optimal policy, which in this problem is a selection of helmet sizes.

The first step is to define a function in such a way that it must give us our desired result. Remember the city block problem; we defined the function $f(x, y)$ as:

$$f(x, y) = \text{the minimum time from } (x, y) \text{ to } B.$$

Work on defining a similar function for our helmet problem.

What about this? Let $f_k(z)$ be defined as:

$f_k(z)$ = the smallest value of average oversizing of soldiers with hat sizes from 6 to z, using k distinct hat sizes.

What is the meaning of

$f_2(7\frac{1}{4})$? _____

$f_3(7\frac{1}{2})$? _____

Does $f_3(6\frac{1}{8})$ make sense? _____

Use the principle of optimality to write the functional equation for $f_k(z)$.

Hint: Repeat in words several times the meaning of the notation $f_k(z)$.

We must choose as one size, hat size z so even those with the largest hat size can be fitted. Let us choose another size x, smaller than z, as a second size. Write an expression for the *least* average oversizing associated with the choices of z and x.

Here is the needed expression:

$$G_x(z) + f_{k-1}(x).$$

Here $G_x(z)$ is the average oversizing for all soldiers fitted with hat size z and $f_{k-1}(x)$ is the minimum oversizing possible when fitting all soldiers with hat size $\leq x$ with $k-1$ distinct hat sizes. But the choice of size x was arbitrary—which is a choice we cannot afford if we are to end up with a truly optimal solution. Write the expression which overcomes this problem.

How about

$$f_k(z) = \underset{\{x\}}{\text{minimum}}[G_x(z) + f_{k-1}(x)]; \quad k = 2, 3.$$

$$f_1(z) = G(z).$$

Help Module B. Optimal Sizing of Steel Beams

Having difficulties?

Do not be discouraged!

Most beginning students are frustrated in applying the principle of optimality. The first step is to write notation for the optimal function:

How about this?

Let $f_k(z)$ represent the least average cost of meeting all demands for beam sizes from 1 to z using k distinct beam sizes.

As usual, this notation looks complicated but all 3 letters are essential to completely describe the problem.

Now try to define mathematically the right-hand side of the relationship

$$f_k(z) = \underline{\hspace{5cm}}.$$

Hint 1: If we must fill requests for beam sizes 1 to z with k distinct sizes, it is obvious that size z must be manufactured.

Hint 2: Let size x be the next smaller size than size z that we choose to manufacture. Once we choose x, we realize that requests for sizes $x + 1$, $x + 2, \ldots, z$ must all be filled with size z. We denote this average cost by $G_x(z)$.

Having so far filled the requests for sizes $x + 1$, $x + 2, \ldots, z$, we are faced with a subproblem of filling requests for sizes $1, \ldots, x$ at least average cost with $k - 1$ sizes. In symbols, this subproblem is denoted by $f_{k-1}(x)$. With these hints, try again to formulate the right-hand side of

$$f_k(z) = \underline{\hspace{5cm}}$$

$$\underline{\hspace{5cm}}.$$

Here it is:

(1)
$$f_k(z) = \underset{\{x\}}{\text{minimum}}[G_x(z) + f_{k-1}(x)]; \quad k = 2, 3,$$

$$f_1(z) = G_1(z).$$

The computations proceed in the same way as for the shrub covering problem. That is,

1. Compute $f_1(z)$ for $z = 1, 2, \ldots, 15$.

2. Then compute $f_2(z)$ for $z = 2, 3, \ldots, 15$ using Equation (1) with $k = 2$.

3. Finally compute $f_3(15)$.

WE RECOMMEND THAT YOU PROCEED TO THE NEXT ASSORTMENT PROBLEM AT THIS TIME. AT SOME LATER TIME, YOU MAY CHOOSE TO CARRY OUT THE CALCULATIONS FOR THE BEAM SIZE PROBLEM.

Help Module C. Optimal Coding of Digitized Photographs

This assortment problem is a bit different from the 3 previous ones. This is not a "sizing" problem. Here a gray level can be assigned to a smaller gray level as well as to a larger one. Recall in our example that x_7 was assigned to x_4. Somehow this notion must be reflected in the formulation of the problem as a dynamic programming problem. Try to do it!

Functional Equation Approach

Your thinking might be as follows:

I want to find an optimal set of 8 gray levels to replace the original set of 64. That is, I want the 8 gray levels that result in the minimum mean square error. Working backwards, I choose the highest of my 8 levels first. Suppose I arbitrarily choose 60. To this level I must assign levels 60, 61, 62, and 63. However, I may also assign levels less than 60 if they are closer to 60 than my second choice. Graphically the choice of gray level 60 would include those levels enclosed in curly brackets 1.

However, if I choose 55 as my next gray level, 59 and 58 would also have to be assigned to gray level 60 since they are closer to 60 than to 55. (Curly brackets 2).

The choice of my third gray level would determine which gray levels would be assigned to 55. If I choose level 48, all gray levels included in the square bracket of the figure would be assigned to level 55.

$\left.\begin{array}{l}63\\62\\61\\60\end{array}\right\}$ 1   Your first selection would be those levels at 60 and above.

$\left.\begin{array}{l}59\\58\end{array}\right\}$ 2   These levels would be added to your first choice, once you have selected 55 as your second level.

$\left.\begin{array}{l}57\\56\\55\\54\\53\\52\end{array}\right]$ These levels would be assigned to level 55.

51

50

49

48

47

⋮

2

1

0

If my next choice is level 41, what levels should be assigned to level 48?

Did you choose levels 51, 50, 49, 48, 47, 46, and 45? This leads me to the following definition:

Let $g_k(w) =$ minimum mean square error of assigning gray levels $0, 1, \ldots, w$ to any of k gray levels among the set $[0, 1, \ldots, w]$ or to level $w + 1$.

The level $w + 1$ is an option because it may be more efficient to assign some gray levels in the set $[0, 1, \ldots, w]$ to $w + 1$ which is the gray level chosen at the preceding stage of the calculation. In effect we really have $k + 1$ gray levels to assign levels $0, 1, \ldots, w$ to, if level $w + 1$ exists. In the final step of computing $g_8(63)$, of course, there is no level $w + 1 = 64$.

Using the principle of optimality, I write

$$g_k(w) = \underset{\{r\}}{\text{minimum}}[E(r, w + 1) + g_{k-1}(r - 1)]; \qquad k = 1, \ldots, 8,$$

where

$$E(r, w+1) = \sum_{j=r+1}^{q} f_j(j-r)^2 + \sum_{j=q+1}^{w} f_j(w+1-j)^2, \qquad r \neq w,$$

$$E(r, w+1) = 0, \qquad r = w,$$

$$E(r, w) = \sum_{j=r+1}^{w} f_j(j-r)^2,$$

and

$$q = r + \left[\text{integer part of } \frac{w+1-r}{2}\right].$$

$E(r, w+1)$ is the mean square error based on assigning all levels from r to w to either the level r or level $w+1$, whichever is closer. The first term

$$\sum_{j=r+1}^{q} f_j(j-r)^2$$

gives the mean square error for all levels assigned to r (all levels closer to it than to $w+1$). The second term

$$\sum_{j=q+1}^{w} f_j(w+1-j)^2$$

gives the mean square error for all levels assigned to $w+1$. The symbol q represents the highest level assigned to level r.

The expression for q is complicated. The following example should help you understand it. If $w+1 = 50$ and $r = 41$, then $q = 41 +$ [integer part of $(50 - 41)/2] = 41 +$ integer part of $4.5 = 45$. Hence gray levels 41, 42, 43, 44, and 45 are assigned to gray level 41 and gray levels 46, 47, 48, and 49 are assigned to gray level 50.

Determine q for the following values of r and $w+1$.

a. $r = 22$, $w+1 = 29$; $q =$ _____.

b. $r = 13$, $w+1 = 16$; $q =$ _____.

c. $r = 40$, $w+1 = 62$; $q =$ _____.

Find 4 gray levels from among 8 levels which minimize mean square error. The fractions of occurrences for the 8 levels are given in Table 1.

Table 1

Level i	Fraction of Occurrence f_i
0	0.05
1	0.10
2	0.10
3	0.15
4	0.35
5	0.05
6	0.15
7	0.05

Table 2

Level w	$g_1(w)$	$r_1(w)$	$g_2(w)$	$r_2(w)$	$g_3(w)$	$r_3(w)$	$g_4(w)$	$r_4(w)$
0	0	0	0		0			
1	0.05	1	0		0			
2	0.15	1	0.05	2	0			
3	0.30	1	0.15	3	0.05	3		
4	0.80	2	0.30	4	0.15	4		
5	1.30	3	0.35	4	0.20	4		
6	1.65	3	0.50	4	0.35	4		
7	3.35	4	1.00	5	0.40	6	0.25	6

Table 2 gives the calculations for the sample problem. As well as computing the optimal value, we also give the optimal policy at each stage, $r_k(w)$. For example, $g_3(4) = 0.15$ is the smallest mean square error for assigning 5 gray levels to level 5 and two other lower levels, and $r_3(4) = 4$ indicates that level 4 is the larger of the two optimal lower levels.

The minimum mean square value is given by $g_4(7) = 0.25$. The optimal 4 levels are 6, 4, 3, 1. We determine this by a tortuous route through the table as follows: We see that $r_4(w) = 6$. We assign levels 6 and 7 to level 6. We must still account for levels 0 to 5. We re-enter the table to obtain $r_3(5) = 4$. This means that levels 4 and 5 are assigned to level 4. We must still account for levels 0 to 3. We re-enter the table to obtain $r_2(3) = 3$. So level 3 is assigned to level 3. Finally, we must account for levels 0 to 2. We re-enter the table to obtain $r_1(2) = 1$. Hence levels 0 to 2 are assigned to level 1.

Summary

You have been exposed to a new and exciting topic in applied mathematics called dynamic programming and have worked on a first-hand level with some real-life problems. In doing this, you experienced the power and simplicity of dynamic programming. You have also seen the limitations of computers in solving certain problems when unsophisticated methods are used. Congratulations on completing this monograph.

The problems described in the monograph are called "multistage decision problems." (Think about how the term "multistage" applies to the problems discussed in the monograph.) Dynamic programming is applicable to many such problems. We have merely scratched the surface in demonstrating the utility of this technique.

Appendix I
Elements of Combinatorics

Factorials

Products such as $5 \cdot 4 \cdot 3 \cdot 2 \cdot 1$ and $10 \cdot 9 \cdot 8 \cdot 7 \cdot 6 \cdot 5 \cdot 4 \cdot 3 \cdot 2 \cdot 1$ are called factorials. Standard notation for such products is 5! and 10!. We read 5! as "5 factorial."
In general for any positive integer n we define $n!$ as follows:

$$n! = n(n - 1)(n - 2) \cdots 1.$$

A special case is made for zero. By definition, $0! = 1$. For example, $4! = 4 \cdot 3 \cdot 2 \cdot 1 = 24$. Evaluate:

1. $3!$ _____

2. $5!$ _____

3. $\dfrac{8!}{4!}$ _____

4. $\dfrac{8!}{4!4!}$ _____

5. $\dfrac{6!}{3!3!}$ _____

6. $(m - n)!$ where $m = 8$, $n = 4$ _____

7. $\dfrac{m!}{(m - n)!}$ where $m = 8$, $n = 4$ _____

8. $\dfrac{m!}{(m - n)!n!}$ where $m = 10$, $n = 5$ _____

The following paragraphs will show how factorials are used to count the number of ways certain events can occur.

Permutations and Combinations

Let's suppose that the letters A and B represent events. In some cases, the order in which these events occur is important. For example, let A and B be defined as:

A: Put on shoes,

B: Tie shoes.

The normal sequence of events, first putting on shoes then tying them, denoted *AB*, could be quite different from (the perhaps painful) *BA*. That is, for these definitions of events $AB \neq BA$.

Suppose, however, that one is making a sandwich and that events *A* and *B* are defined as:

A: Place bologna on bread,

B: Place cheese on bread.

It makes little difference to the eater whether the bologna or cheese was first placed on the bread. In this case, we can consider that $AB = BA$.

Let's now make choices of 1, 2, or 3 events from 3 events, called *A*, *B*, and *C*. In some cases, order is important and in others, order is not considered important. The possible choices are listed in Table A-1. Carefully study the entries in the table.

Table A-1
All Possible Selections

Number of Events Chosen	Order not important (Combinations)	Order important (Permutations)
1	*A, B, C*	*A, B, C*
2	*AB, AC, BC*	*AB, BA, AC, CA, BC, CB*
3	*ABC*	*ABC, ACB, BAC, BCA, CAB, CBA*

The selections made in which *order* is *not important* are called *combinations*. Selections in which *order* is *important* are called *permutations*. These two concepts are widely used in many areas of applied mathematics.

Clearly, we can't write out such lists each time we want to know how many permutations or combinations are possible. (For example, the question: "In how many distinct ways can we form sets of 3 initials from the 26 letters of the alphabet in which no letter is repeated?" would require a very long list.) What's needed are formulae to compute the numbers of such permutations and combinations when making selections.

Suppose one is interested in permutations, that is, *order is important.* How many ways are there of selecting 2 letters at a time from *A, B,* and *C*—no letter being repeated in any single permutation? (That is *AA, BB* or *CC* are not allowed.) To answer the question, think of the two spaces into which the two letters of each permutation will be placed:

_____   _____

We will count the number of ways each space can be filled, putting that number into the space. The product of the resulting numbers then will give us the needed answer. (Convince yourself that this is so!)

In the first space, we can put any of the 3 letters *A, B* or *C*. So we have

___3___   _____

However, once we choose a letter for the first space, we have only 2 choices left for the second space because no single letter can occupy both spots. This gives:

___3___   ___2___

The product of these numbers, namely six, is the number of ways to fill the two spaces—when order is important and allowing no repeated letters in one permutation. Note that this result agrees with the number of permutations found in row 2 of Table A-1:

$$AB, \ BA, \ AC, \ CA, \ BC, \ CB.$$

One writes the above result as $P(3,2) = 6$.

How many permutations are there of the letters A, B, and C taken 3 at a time? As before, think of 3 spaces—which are the places of the letters in each permutation. The first space can be filled in 3 ways, that is with A, B or C. The second space can now be filled with either of the two remaining letters. With the first two spaces filled, the last can be filled only with the one letter remaining, so we have:

$$\underline{\quad 3 \quad} \qquad \underline{\quad 2 \quad} \qquad \underline{\quad 1 \quad}$$

Therefore, there are $3 \cdot 2 \cdot 1 = 6$ permutations of the $\underline{3}$ letters A, B, and C taken $\underline{3}$ at a time, allowing no repeated letters in any permutation. We denote this quantity $P(3,3)$ for short. The exact permutations are shown in row 3 of Table A-1.

$$ABC, \ ACB, \ BAC, \ BCA, \ CAB, \ CBA.$$

Some other examples of permutation calculations and notation are:
The number of permutations of 4 things taken 2 at a time:

$$P(4,2) = \underline{4} \ \underline{3} = 12.$$

The number of permutations of 5 things taken 4 at a time:

$$P(5,4) = \underline{5} \ \underline{4} \ \underline{3} \ \underline{2} = 120.$$

The number of permutations of 6 things taken 1 at a time:

$$P(6,1) = \underline{6} = 6.$$

Evaluate:

9. $P(7,4)$ _____

10. $P(8,5)$ _____

11. How many sets of three initials can be formed from the 26 letters of the alphabet if no letter may be repeated? _____

12. How many license plates consisting of 5 digits can be made if no digit may be repeated? _____

From the previous examples and problems you may notice the following form of the calculation:

(A.1) $\qquad P(M,N) = \underbrace{M(M-1)(M-2)\cdots(M-N+1)}_{N \text{ Factors}}.$

In fact, the above is a general expression for $P(M,N)$. But, by multiplying top and bottom of the right-hand side of the equation above by $(M-N)!$, we obtain:

$$P(M,N) = \frac{M(M-1)(M-2)\cdots(M-N+1)\cdot(M-N)!}{(M-N)!}.$$

The equation above can be simplified to

(A.2)
$$P(M, N) = \frac{M!}{(M - N)!}.$$

Equation (A.2) is the commonly used expression for $P(M, N)$.

13. Using equation (A.2), find $P(7, 4)$ and $P(8, 5)$. Compare with your answers in 9 and 10.

$P(7, 4)$ _____ $P(8, 5)$ _____

But counting combinations is also useful. (Especially if you open a sandwich shop!) Consider the second row of Table A-1:

Number of Events Chosen	Order Not Important	Order Important
2	AB, AC, BC	AB, BA, AC, CA, BC, CB

Note that each *combination* of 2 distinct letters yields 2 permutations. For example:

Combination	Associated Permutations
AB	AB, BA
AC	AC, CA
BC	BC, CB

This fact follows from equation (A.2), which tells us that from any selection of N distinct things taken N at a time we have $N!$ permutations, that is:

(A.3)
$$P(N, N) = \frac{N!}{(N - N)!} = \frac{N!}{0!} = \frac{N!}{1} = N!.$$

Now let $C(M, N)$ represent the number of combinations of M things taken N at a time. Then, from equation (A.3), it can be seen that:

$$C(M, N) \cdot N! = P(M, N)$$

or

$$C(M, N) = \frac{P(M, N)}{N!}.$$

Using equation (A.2), this expression can be rewritten as

(A.4)
$$C(M, N) = \frac{M!}{(M - N)!N!}.$$

$C(M, N)$ is often written as simply $\binom{M}{N}$.

Evaluate:

14. $C(5, 3)$ _____

15. $C(8, 5)$ _____

16. An exam consists of 10 questions, and a student is told to select 7. How many different selections does this student have? _____

17. An exam consists of 10 questions. A student is told to answer the first three questions and then answer four of the remaining questions. How many different selections does this student have? _____

An additional complication arises when not all objects one is selecting from are unique. For example, how many permutations are there of the 4 letters in the following set: $\{A, A, B, B\}$. If all the events in the set were unique, then the number of permutations would be (equation (A.3)) $4! = 24$. But clearly, the first two events in the set are the same, and the last two events are as well. There are in fact only 6 distinct permutations of the four letters and they are listed below:

$$AABB \qquad BBAA$$
$$ABBA \qquad BAAB$$
$$ABAB \qquad BABA$$

If the 4 events were distinct, four $(2! \cdot 2!)$ permutations of each of the 6 above would be possible, namely 2! for permuting the two A's and 2! for permuting the two B's, giving the required total of 24.

Thus, when permuting M objects of which M_1 are of one kind (say A's) and M_2 are of another kind (say B's) $(M_1 + M_2 = M)$, the number of permutations is given by:

(A.5)
$$\frac{(M_1 + M_2)!}{M_1! \cdot M_2!}$$

18. How many permutations are there of the letters *AAABBBB*? _____

19. How many permutations are there of the letters *NNNEEE*? _____

In the context of our $M \times M$ shortest path problem, we have paths with $2M$ steps, M of which are to be East steps and M of which are to be North steps. The number of distinct paths is exactly the number of *permutations* of $2M$ objects (E's and N's) of which M are E's and M are N's. From the expression in (A.5), the desired number of permutations (paths) is

$$\frac{(2M)!}{M! \cdot M!}.$$

For example, problem 23 asks you to estimate the number of paths in a 10×10 shortest path problem. This may be found by computing

$$\frac{20!}{10! \cdot 10!} = 184,756.$$

Make use of a calculator in solving the following:

20. How many distinct paths can be found in a 4×4 shortest path problem?

_____

21. How many distinct paths can be found in a 7×7 shortest path problem?

_____

22. How many distinct paths can be found in a 30×30 shortest path problem?

_____

Appendix II
A Short Biography of
Richard Earnest Bellman

Richard Earnest Bellman, the inventor of dynamic programming, was born on August 26, 1920 in New York City. He remained in New York during his youth and in 1941 graduated from Brooklyn College with a Bachelor of Arts Degree in Mathematics. He went on to graduate school at the Johns Hopkins University but later transferred and received his Master's Degree in Mathematics from the University of Wisconsin. During this period Bellman taught undergraduate courses forty-two hours a week, seven hours a day, six days a week. He worked on his own graduate courses at night and spent an average of twenty hours a day on mathematics. In 1946 he was awarded his Ph. D. in Mathematics by Princeton University. The topic of his dissertation was Stability Theory.[1]

Part of Dr. Bellman's career was spent teaching in the university environment. For two years following his graduation from Princeton Dr. Bellman remained there as an Assistant Professor of Mathematics. From 1948 to 1952 he was an Associate Professor of Mathematics at Stanford University and during the 1956 academic year was a visiting Professor of Engineering at the University of California at Los Angeles. At the time of his death on March 19, 1984, Dr. Bellman was Professor of Mathematics, Electrical Engineering, and Medicine at the University of Southern California, having joined that faculty in 1965.

Other times during his career important problems and projects of society consumed his energies. Several war years were spent at the Los Alamos Scientific Laboratory, which was then engaged in the development of the atomic bomb. PFC (Private First Class) Bellman reported to Los Alamos in 1943 and balked at the repetitive "unthinking" calculating work he had been given. To silence the "uppity" graduate student, Bellman was given an important problem, one which could not be solved by any of the top physicists of Los Alamos, and was told not to return until his solution was complete. The problem was to solve an equation which would be used to predict the intensity of the bomb blast as a function of the distance from the burst. Within 10 minutes Bellman had resolved the problem, stunning all the top physicists. From that moment on Richard Bellman's talents were more fully utilized at Los Alamos.

In 1951–52 he returned to Princeton University to participate in Project Matterhorn, the development of the hydrogen bomb. He and many other scientists who worked on the project originally considered the development of such a weapon to be impossible. They accepted the work in the hope that they would reach just that conclusion. As is now well known, however, the theoretical basis

---

[1]The effect on the stability of systems (usually described by differential equations) when acted upon by some external force.

for the bomb is very simple, something that many capable graduate students could derive.

From 1952–65 Bellman was employed be the RAND (Research and New Development) Corporation. "Game theory" was a major area of emphasis in the RAND Mathematics Division. This is the mathematical theory of competition, and it was expected to be of great use in the evaluation and development of military strategy.

It was during these travels to Princeton, Los Alamos, and the RAND Corporation that Bellman met and was influenced by John von Neumann, another great contemporary mathematician. In fact Bellman's book *Applied Dynamic Programming* is dedicated: "To the memory of John von Neumann, Inspiration and Friend."

From 1969–75 Bellman was affiliated with the Center for the Study of Democratic Institutions. This is an organization which seeks to make democracy work by promoting the exchange of ideas. Persons from varying fields, holding different opinions, meet to discuss contemporary issues, e.g., war and peace, racial problems, etc. Bellman's work at the Center was titled "Retrospective Futurology," meaning to try to predict what the future holds by analyzing what has happened in the past.

Bellman's work, throughout his career, was "applied" in nature. He developed methods and techniques in response to the need for solutions to real-world problems, which range over a wide variety of fields. He also concentrated on developing his techniques and concepts in a way which makes the necessary computations feasible and efficient on modern digital computers.

To a large extent, Bellman's mathematical solutions seemed to be derived from three main concepts: (1) dynamic programming, (2) invariant imbedding, and (3) fuzzy sets or systems. A brief description of each concept follows:

Dynamic programming is a mathematical method for solving problems in which a large number of decisions must be made, often sequentially. The objective is usually to make that set of decisions which maximizes or minimizes some desired quantity such as profit realized or time required. Such problems are termed "multistage decision processes."

Invariant imbedding is a mathematical technique in which a specific problem is viewed and solved as being one of a family of related but more general problems. The benefit of this approach is that the problem solution is often greatly eased because of a resulting simplification of problem conditions.

Fuzzy systems (or sets) are not mathematical techniques but rather concepts. A fuzzy system is one whose defining properties or status is not known with certainty. (A fuzzy set is one whose elements are not known with certainty.)

Bellman applied these concepts to problems which arise in many fields. Following is a sampling of the contributions he made to the applied sciences.

The application of mathematics and engineering to medical problems was one of Dr. Bellman's main areas of interest. He worked on the application of dynamic programming to health systems, including the optimum allocation of resources to ongoing medical research and development activities. Also, because of his realization that an increasing number of mathematicians, physicists, and engineers wanted to work in the fields of medicine and physiology, Bellman published the book *An Introduction to Mathematical Methods in Medicine*. The theme of this book is how to develop the computational procedures—not just the theory—required to solve specific medical problems.

For example, one topic considered in this book is the so-called "side-effect" problem. In it, the patient's physiological subsystems are considered as compartments. The objective is to maintain a therapeutic level of a drug in certain compartments while avoiding too high a concentration in other compartments where dangerous side effects could occur. It is shown how dynamic programming furnishes a quick and easy computational solution to this particular problem.

A second volume on *Mathematics in Medicine* was primarily concerned with tumor locations and radiation dosimetry.[2] Tumor location is described as a generalized search problem and is also attacked through the use of dynamic programming. The radiation dosimetry problem is considered by means of the invariant imbedding technique. The emphasis is on the computational aspects because the actual clinical applications of the results are of paramount importance. Dr. Bellman's interest in this particular topic stems, in part, from the fact that his mother died of cancer when he was 18 years old.

With respect to mathematics in medicine, Dr. Bellman stated that:

What will be clear is how much remains to be done. In any direction, more realistic models are required. Thus, this is an ideal field for the young mathematician.

The field of solar energy is another area to which Dr. Bellman responded. He wrote two volumes on the application of the invariant imbedding technique to radiative transfer. This work is fundamental to the mathematical treatment of the increasingly important field of solar energy utilization.

Further, Dr. Bellman's expertise in the subject of fuzzy systems led to the application of mathematics to the social sciences. Specific areas of application include: work/family interaction, deciphering of ancient languages, the conduct and evaluation of psychiatric interviews, and psychotherapy.

In addition, Dr. Bellman's necessary interest in computing, and perhaps his interaction with von Neumann, led him to examinations of artificial intelligence. In his book on this area he examined such questions as: Can computers think and exhibit "rational" behavior?; and Is it possible to develop mathematical models of the mind? The latter topic was, in fact, one of the last areas of interest to von Neumann.

In order to pass his experience and insight to future mathematicians, Dr. Bellman, with Dr. E. Stanley Lee, prepared a series of volumes on *what the young analyst should know*. Volume subjects include: *Basic Techniques* (this volume includes dynamic programming and invariant imbedding), *Partial Differential Equations, Laplace Transforms, Fuzzy Systems, Simulation, The Identification of Systems*, and *Stochastic Processes*.

Dr. Bellman's outstanding work earned him many awards. Included among them are the following: the First Norbert Weiner Prize in Applied Mathematics given by the American Mathematical Society and the Society of Industrial and Applied Mathematics (1970); the First Dickson Prize, awarded by Carnegie Mellon University (1970); Fellowship in the American Academy of Arts and Sciences (1975); the Second Annual John von Neumann Theory Award by the Institute of Management Sciences and the Operations Research Society of America (1976).

---

[2]Radiation dosimetry is the study of the radiation dosages and schedules required for the treatment of malignancies of various types.

He received the 1979 Institute of Electrical and Electronics Engineers Medal of Honor, which bears the following inscription:

> *For contributions to decision processes and control system theory, particularly the creation and application of Dynamic Programming.*

This award carried with it a $10,000 prize. Dr. Bellman was later nominated and endorsed by hundreds of his colleagues for the National Medal of Science.

While the works and awards of Richard Bellman listed in this article are highly impressive, they are only the tip of the iceberg. At the time of his death, Dr. Bellman had to his credit over 600 published research papers, 44 books, and 7 monographs. In addition he was the founder and editor of the *Journal of Mathematical Analysis and Applications*, as well as an editor of the Academic Press *Series on Mathematics in Science and Engineering*.

Appendix III
On Binary Numbers

The binary number 101101 is interpreted as follows:

$$\begin{array}{cccccc}
1 & 0 & 1 & 1 & 0 & 1 \\
\uparrow & \uparrow & \uparrow & \uparrow & \uparrow & \uparrow \\
32\text{'s} & 16\text{'s} & 8\text{'s} & 4\text{'s} & 2\text{'s} & 1\text{'s}
\end{array}$$

$= 32 + 0 + 8 + 4 + 0 + 1 = 45$. So 45 is the decimal number equivalent to the binary number 101101.

The binary number $110011 = 32 + 16 + 0 + 0 + 2 + 1 = 51$.

The binary number $001111 = 0 + 0 + 8 + 4 + 2 + 1 = 15$.

1. Find the decimal number equivalents of the following binary numbers:

$$101010 = \underline{\hspace{3cm}}.$$
$$000010 = \underline{\hspace{3cm}}.$$
$$111111 = \underline{\hspace{3cm}}.$$

In digital computers and communication systems, it turns out to be quite convenient to operate with a scale of two rather than a scale of ten. This means that every number which we usually write in the scale of ten must be converted into the scale of two before digital computers or communication systems can do their tasks. In a computer, a zero can be interpreted as a current not going through a component, while a one can be interpreted as a current going through a component. In other words, a zero represents an "off" and a one represents an "on."

In a communication system, a zero can be sent as a positive pulse and a one as a negative pulse. Hence, binary numbers result in simplified designs of computers and communication systems.

Special Projects

1. Write computer programs to solve general problems of:
   a. Shortest path
   b. Shrub covering
   c. Helmet sizing
   d. Steel beam sizing
   e. Coding of digitized photographs

2. Using the data given in the monographs, find:
   a. The best 3 helmet sizes
   b. The best 3 steel beam sizes

3. For the digitized photograph problem, pick values for the f_i $(i = 1, 2, \ldots, 64)$ and find the best 3 gray levels. Note: The sum of the f_i's should be 1.00.

References

R. Bellman and S. Dreyfus, *Applied Dynamic Programming*, Princeton University Press, Princeton, N.J., 1962.

W. Sodowski, "A few remarks on the Assortment Problem," *Management Science*, Vol. 6, No. 1, 1959.

D. J. White, *Dynamic Programming*, Holden-Day, 1969.

D. Goulet and W. Sacco, "Algorithms for Sizing Helmets," Ballistics Research Laboratory (APG, MD) Memorandum Report 30, 1971.

Answers

Answers to Exercises

1. 3.1536×10^7 seconds/year

2. 3.1536×10^{12} additions/year; 3.1536×10^{14} additions/century; 3.1536×10^{15} additions/1000 years; 3.1536×10^{18} additions/million years

3. 14 minutes

4. ENEN   23 minutes
   EENN   25 minutes
   NNEE   15 minutes
   ENNE   20 minutes
   NEEN   17 minutes

5. NENE

6. 14 minutes

7. 2

8. 2

9. 3

10. ENNNEE   27
    ENNENE   27
    ENNEEN   33
    NENENE   21
    NENEEN   27

11. NNNEEE

12. 6

13. 3

14. 3

15. 5

16. 100

17. Your answer

18. 20

19. 10

20. 10

21. Your answer

22. 19

23. Your answer. The correct answer is 184,756.

24. $184,756 \times 19 = 3,510,364$

25. About 35 seconds

26. 59

27. 1.183×10^{17}

28. $59 \times (1.183 \times 10^{17}) = 6.9797 \times 10^{18}$

29. 6.9799×10^{18} seconds or 2.213×10^6 years, which is more than 2 million years.

30. East

31. 13 minutes

32. NENE, 14 minutes

33. Yes

34. NNEEE

35. NEEEENNN or ENEEENNN

36. Any path with three East and three North steps in the first six steps taken will pass through G.

37. 40

38. 17

39. 13

40. 1

41. 6

42. 10

43.
$$f(1,0) = \text{minimum}\{t_E(1,0) + f(2,0);$$
$$t_N(1,0) + f(1,1)\}$$
$$= \text{minimum}\{22; 17\} = 17$$

44.
$$f(0,0) = \text{minimum}\{t_E(0,0) + f(1,0);$$
$$t_N(0,0) + f(0,1)\}$$
$$= \text{minimum}\{20; 14\} = 14$$

45. No. Since $C_1 < C_2 < \cdots < C_{10}$, it is to your advantage to use as many sizes as you are allowed.

46. a) Cost of policy $(10, 5, 3) =$
$$5C_{10} + 2C_5 + 3C_3 =$$
$$5(21) + 2(8) + 3(5) = \$136$$

b) 10, 4, 3 ... $148
10, 4, 2 ... 148
10, 4, 1 ... 148
10, 3, 2 ... 160
10, 3, 1 ... 158
10, 2, 1 ... 173

47. Policy (10,7,5) has the smallest associated cost.

48. No

49. The least cost of covering shrub 1 with one cover.

50. The least cost of covering shrubs 1, 2, 3 with covers of one size.

51. The least cost of covering shrubs 1, 2, 3, 4, 5 with covers of two sizes.

52. No

53. Yes

54. 1

55. $120

56. .28125

57. $G(6\frac{5}{8}) = .0475$
$G_{6\frac{5}{8}}(7\frac{1}{4}) = .10125$
$G_{7\frac{1}{4}}(8) = .1325$

58. See Help Module A

59. See Help Module B

60. See Help Module C

Answers to Questions in Help Modules

Help Module A

$f_2(7\frac{1}{4})$ is the smallest value of the average oversizing of soldiers with hat sizes from 6 to $7\frac{1}{4}$ using two distinct hat sizes.

$f_3(7\frac{1}{2})$ is the smallest value of the average oversizing of soldiers with hat sizes from 6 to $7\frac{1}{2}$ using three distinct hat sizes.

$f_3(6\frac{1}{8})$ does not make sense. We do not need 3 sizes for only two sizes of heads.

Help Module C

a. $r = 22$, $w + 1 = 29$; $q = 25$
b. $r = 13$, $w + 1 = 16$; $q = 14$
c. $r = 40$, $w + 1 = 62$; $q = 51$

Answers to Questions in the Appendices

Appendix I

1. 6

2. 120

3. 1680

4. 70

5. 20

6. 24

7. 1680

8. 252

9. 840

10. 6720

11. 15,600

12. 30, 240

13. $P(7, 4) = 840$; $P(8, 5) = 6720$

14. 10

15. 56

16. 120

17. 35

18. 35

19. 20

20. 70

21. 3432

22. 1.183×10^{17}

Appendix III

1. $101010 = 42$

2. $000010 = 2$

3. $111111 = 63$